When the Light Hurts

A Quiet Companion for the Darkest Days of Depression

Angie G. Ford

Sunflower Phoenix Publishing

ISBN: 979-8-9959413-4-7

Published by Sunflower Phoenix Publishing

This book is not a substitute for professional medical advice, diagnosis, or treatment. If you are in crisis, please call or text 988, contact emergency services, or go to the nearest emergency room.

For anyone who is tired of being told to look on the bright side.

I am writing this from beside you, in the dark.

Table of Contents

Introduction: I Know This Place

There is a specific kind of darkness that cannot be explained to someone who has never lived inside it. It is not the darkness of a bad day, or a passing sadness, or a temporary grief. It is a thick, heavy, suffocating silence that settles into your bones and convinces you that the light is never coming back.

If you are holding this book, you probably know exactly what I am talking about.

I know this place. I have lived in it. I have felt the vacuum in my chest, the concrete in my legs, and the exhaustion of simply trying to exist when my own mind was telling me I was a burden to everyone I loved. I know what it is like to stare at the ceiling and calculate how many people I was going to disappoint that day, before my feet even touched the floor.

I also know what it is like to stand on the outside of that darkness, watching someone I love disappear into it. I have been the person drowning, and I have been the person standing on the shore, throwing life preservers that only felt like anvils to the person I was trying to save.

I have lived on both sides of this fence.

When I was in the dark, the last thing I wanted was someone standing in the bright sunlight, shouting down at me to 'just look on the bright side' or 'just snap out of it.' Those words did not feel like help. They felt like an accusation. They made me feel more broken, more isolated, and more convinced that I was failing at being a functioning human being.

That is why this book is not going to do that.

This book is not an action plan. It is not a ten-step program to a happier life. It is not going to ask you to suddenly become the sun when you feel like you are made of stone.

This book is simply a companion. It is a hand on your shoulder in the dark.

I am writing this to offer you my experience, my strength, and my hope. But I am not offering it from a pedestal. I am offering it from the chair right next to yours.

I want to validate the reality of what you are going through. I want to give you language for the physical and emotional exhaustion of depression, so that you know you are not making it up, and you are not alone.

We are going to talk about why the dark starts to feel like home. We are going to talk about the mask you wear to survive, and the lies your depression tells you in your own voice. We are going to talk about why well-meaning help often feels like pressure, and why hope can sometimes feel like an assault.

And eventually, we will talk about one small, clean signal you can send to yourself to interrupt the static.

But we are not going to rush.

You do not have to fix everything today. You do not have to fix anything today.

For now, just know this: I know this place. You are not alone. And it is okay if the only thing you do today is keep breathing.

Let's just sit here for a while.

Chapter 1: When the Nightmare Does Not Stop

The Intrusion of Morning

How does a day start when the nightmare has not stopped?

For most people, waking up is a reset. The sun rises, the alarm goes off, and a new day begins with a clean slate. Morning is supposed to be a transition from the quiet of sleep into the possibility of waking life. It is the time of coffee brewing, plans forming, and energy slowly returning to the body after a long rest.

But when depression has settled into your bones, waking up is not a beginning.

It is an intrusion.

You open your eyes, and the heavy, familiar weight is already there, pressing down on your chest before your feet even touch the floor. You stare at the ceiling. The paint texture is familiar. The angle of light coming through the blinds is familiar. And the dread that washes over you is entirely familiar.

In those first ten minutes awake, before you have formed a single coherent thought about your schedule or your obligations, the physical reality of the day announces itself. Your body feels like it has been filled with wet concrete overnight. The thought of moving, of participating in the world, feels like an enormous, unreasonable request.

You lie there, listening to the alarm buzz on the nightstand. You know you should reach out and turn it off. You know the sound is grating. But even extending your arm requires a negotiation with gravity that you are not prepared to make.

You are technically awake, but that is not the same as living.

You are simply existing in a haze of consciousness, trapped between the relief of unconsciousness and the demanding glare of the morning.

This is one of the cruelest parts of depression: the immediate realization that nothing has changed. Sleep did not fix it. Rest did not restore you. You survived another night only to be handed another day you do not feel equipped to carry.

The nightmare did not end when you opened your eyes.

It simply moved from your dreams into your bedroom.

A State of Being, Not a Mood

This is the reality of a dark day.

It is not just sadness.

Sadness is an emotion that moves through you. It arrives, it peaks, and eventually, it passes. Sadness is often a response to something that happened: a loss, a disappointment, a heartbreak, a moment of pain. Sadness cries, and then, eventually, sadness rests.

Sadness is a visitor in your house.

Depression is different.

Depression is not a visitor. It is the house itself.

Depression is a state of being that holds you still. It does not simply move through you. It moves into you and changes the architecture of your mind. It alters the way you perceive time, the way you experience physical space, and the way you process love.

It is a vacuum pulling at your ribs, a physical ache that eventually goes numb. You might feel like a marionette, with some outside force moving your limbs while inside, everything is silent and completely empty. You may not be crying. You may not be grieving in any obvious way. You may simply be enduring the profound absence of feeling.

People who have not experienced this kind of darkness often misunderstand it.

They think depression is a bad mood that lasted too long. They think you need motivation, a change of scenery, or a gentle push to get moving. They suggest a funny movie, a nice dinner, a walk outside, or a reminder to look on the bright side.

They may mean well. But they do not understand the sheer physical and mental effort it takes just to exist when your mind is telling you that you are entirely alone and utterly useless.

They do not understand that you cannot simply "snap out of" a state of being that has changed how you process reality.

You cannot repair a structural collapse with a positive thought.

The Mountains of Daily Life

On a dark day, the world outside your window feels aggressively loud and painfully bright. The obligations of daily life seem monumental. They are not just chores. They are mountains you have no strength to climb.

A phone buzzes on the nightstand.

To someone else, it is just a message from a friend checking in. To you, it is a demand for energy you do not possess. It is the pressure to sound normal, to craft a response that proves you are functioning, to offer the right amount of warmth without letting too much truth slip through.

So you let it buzz.

And as the screen goes dark, the guilt settles in. It whispers that you are a terrible friend. It tells you that you are slowly pushing everyone away. It turns one unanswered message into evidence that you are failing at being loved.

A glass of water sits across the room.

You know you should drink it. Your throat is dry, and your head aches from dehydration. But the distance between the bed and the dresser feels impossible. Sitting up, swinging your legs over the edge, and standing requires a negotiation with gravity that you are too tired to win.

So you stay thirsty.

And the thirst becomes just another quiet punishment.

You hear people moving around in the rest of the house. Footsteps in the hallway. A cabinet closing in the kitchen. The faint sound of someone beginning their day.

To anyone else, these might be comforting sounds of a shared life. To you, they feel like threats. They are reminders that other people are functioning, that the world is moving forward, and that at any moment, someone might knock on your door and ask you to join it.

Even the thought of eating becomes an exhausting calculation.

Making food requires decisions. It requires standing in the kitchen, opening the refrigerator, looking at ingredients, and combining them into something that counts as a meal. When your brain is running on emergency power, the cognitive load of making a sandwich can feel like solving a complex equation.

So you do not eat.

Or you eat whatever requires zero preparation, not because you are not hungry, but because you cannot afford the energy it takes to feed yourself.

Showering feels impossible too.

It is not just turning on the water. It is taking off your clothes. It is feeling the cold air. It is standing up for ten minutes. It is washing. Drying. Finding clean clothes. Putting them on. Every single step is a hurdle, and each hurdle is taller than it should be.

And so, the mountains remain unclimbed.

You remain in bed, staring at the ceiling, while the day keeps moving without you.

The Arithmetic of Disappointment

While your body lies still, your mind is racing.

It is calculating how many people you will disappoint today.

It is running a ledger of every mistake, every missed opportunity, every flaw. It is a quiet, devastating arithmetic that always ends with the same conclusion:

You are a burden, and the world is moving on without you.

Before you have even thrown off the covers, you have already tallied up the day's failures.

You failed to wake up with energy.

You failed to answer the text message.

You failed to take a shower.

You failed to eat something real.

You failed to be the partner, the parent, the friend, the employee, the sibling, or the person you believe you are supposed to be.

This arithmetic is relentless. It does not allow for grace. It does not account for the fact that you are fighting an invisible war. It only looks at the outward results: the unmade bed, the unanswered phone, the silence, the stillness.

Then it declares you guilty.

It tells you that your inability to function is not a symptom of an illness, but a moral failure. It tells you that if you just tried harder, if you just cared more, if you were stronger, you would already be up and moving.

And because you are not up and moving, it concludes that you do not care.

This is what the dark looks like.

It is not always dramatic or cinematic. It is not always sobbing on the bathroom floor or screaming into a pillow. Sometimes it is the quiet, crushing weight of a Tuesday morning when the simplest things feel like lifting stones, and your own mind has opened a case against you before the day has even begun.

The Relief of Evening

And so, you wait.

You wait for the day to end so you can close your eyes again.

The evening brings a small measure of relief, not because you feel better, but because the world stops asking things of you. The sun goes down, and with it, the expectation that you should be productive. The emails stop arriving. The texts slow down. The pressure to be out in the world, participating in the bright and busy lives of other people, finally recedes.

When it is dark outside, it feels more acceptable to be dark inside.

You can retreat into the shadows without having to explain yourself or perform normalcy for anyone else's comfort.

Nighttime may be the only time when your internal state seems to match the external world. The stillness of the house is no longer a reminder of what you are failing to do. It is simply the natural order of things. For a few hours, you are allowed to exist quietly, hidden away from the demands of a life you cannot currently manage.

There can be a strange comfort in knowing that everyone else is asleep.

While they are unconscious, they cannot need anything from you. They cannot ask how you are doing. They cannot look at you with that painful mixture of pity, confusion, worry, and frustration that you have come to dread.

For a little while, no one is expecting you to become a person they can understand.

But even this relief is not clean.

Evening is softened by the knowledge that morning will come again. The sun will rise. The alarm will sound. The world will begin asking things of you before you have had a chance to become ready.

The intrusion of morning is always waiting.

The relief of evening is only a temporary pause in the nightmare.

It Is Enough to Be Here

If this is where you are right now, I want you to hear this clearly:

You are not lazy.

You are not weak.

You are carrying an invisible, crushing weight, and the fact that you are still breathing under it is a testament to your endurance, even if it does not feel that way.

I am not going to offer you a pep talk. I am not going to tell you that tomorrow will be better. I am not going to tell you that you just need to change your mindset.

When you are in the middle of the nightmare, those words do not help. They only make you feel more alone.

Instead, I am just going to sit here with you.

You do not need to apologize for the days when the dark is too heavy. You do not need to perform normalcy for anyone else's comfort. You do not need to prove your worth by being productive.

You are allowed to be tired.

You are allowed to be empty.

You are allowed to understand why staying in bed feels like the only possible thing when the gravity of the world is too strong to fight.

Right now, it is enough to still be here.

If all you can do today is keep breathing under the weight of it, that still counts as being here.

And for this page, for this moment, you do not have to be here by yourself.

For Today

Right now, it is enough to still be here.

You do not have to be here by yourself.

Chapter 2: Why the Dark Starts to Feel Like Home

The Dark Is Not Comfort, But It Is Familiar

The dark is not comfortable.

Let us be honest about that right from the beginning. It is important that we do not romanticize this space.

It is heavy. It is isolating. It is a suffocating weight pressing against your ribs, making the simple act of drawing a full breath feel like an athletic event. It is not a place you would choose to live if you believed there was somewhere else you could safely breathe.

But after a while, the dark becomes familiar.

And familiar, even when it is painful, can start to feel like the closest thing to safe.

When you have lived in the dark long enough, you learn its rhythms. You know what to expect from it. The ache in your chest is constant, but it is a known ache. The numbness is heavy, but it is a known heaviness. The dark does not surprise you. It does not ask you to perform. It does not expect anything from you that you are not already giving.

The outside world is unpredictable.

A conversation can suddenly turn into an argument. A task at work can suddenly become overwhelming. A beautiful sunny day can suddenly make you feel intensely, unbearably guilty for not enjoying it. The world is full of variables you cannot control, full of sudden shifts in emotional weather that you do not have the energy to navigate.

The dark, by comparison, has fewer variables.

It is predictable.

And when your nervous system is completely exhausted, when you are running on the bare minimum of emotional fuel, predictability can feel like refuge.

Known Pain Feels Safer Than Unknown Hope

There is a strange and terrible comfort in suffering that at least feels predictable.

Think about the physical sensation of depression. It often feels like a heavy blanket pulled tightly over your head. The blanket is suffocating, yes. It is hard to breathe under it. It blocks out the light and muffles the sound of the world.

But it also forms a barrier..

It holds you in place.

It becomes a grip you learn to lean into.

When you are under that blanket, the bright, loud, demanding world of normal life feels terrifying. That world is full of unknowns. It is full of people who might ask you questions you do not have the energy to answer. It is full of obligations you do not have the strength to meet. It is full of the possibility of failure, and the possibility of letting someone down.

Hope, in that state, is not always a comfort.

Hope can feel like a threat.

Hope asks you to throw off the heavy blanket, stand up, and walk into a world where you might fail, where you might be hurt again, where the pain might catch you by surprise.

Known pain is a terrible roommate, but it is one you know how to live with. You have built a tolerance for it. You know exactly how much it hurts, and you know that you can survive it because you are surviving it right now.

Unknown hope feels like standing at the edge of a cliff and being asked to jump into the fog.

Why would you jump when you are already on the ground, even if the ground is cold and hard?

When Numbness Becomes a Shelter

Eventually, the sharp pain of depression often gives way to something else.

Numbness.

Numbness is the body's emergency defense. When the emotional pain becomes too loud, too sharp, too constant to endure, the nervous system turns the volume down. You stop feeling the sharp ache, but you also stop feeling everything else. The joy, the connection, the warmth, the small pleasures that used to reach you, they all fade into a flat, gray static.

To the outside world, this numbness can look like apathy.

It can look like you do not care.

People may become frustrated with you. They may accuse you of being indifferent to their feelings or detached from your own life. They might say you are being selfish, or that you have simply stopped trying.

They do not understand that the apathy is not a choice.

It is a circuit breaker that tripped to keep the whole system from catching fire.

From the inside, numbness feels like shelter.

It is a thick wall of glass between you and the world.

When you are numb, nothing can fully touch you. A friend cancels plans? It does not matter. You make a mistake at work? It does not matter. The world is burning? It does not matter.

The numbness protects you from the sharp edges of life. It wraps you in a thick layer of cotton so the impacts of daily existence do not bruise you quite as deeply.

Leaving the dark means risking that glass breaking.

It means allowing yourself to feel again.

And when the last thing you felt was unbearable pain, why would you want to shatter the only thing that seems to be keeping you safe?

The Relief of Not Performing

There is another reason the dark starts to feel like home.

It is the only place where you do not have to pretend.

When you are out in the world, you are constantly managing other people's expectations. You are smiling when you do not want to smile. You are answering "I am fine" when you are crumbling. You are spending enormous amounts of energy just to appear normal so that no one worries, no one asks questions, and no one tries to fix you.

But in the dark, in the quiet of your room, with the door closed and the lights off, the performance ends.

You do not have to be okay.

You do not have to be productive.

You do not have to manage anyone else's feelings.

You can simply exist as a person in pain, resting in the only place that does not demand more from you than you have.

That relief is profound. It is a genuine exhale.

When you finally close the bedroom door and let the mask drop, the relief is almost physical. Your shoulders lower. Your jaw unclenches. You stop policing your own facial expressions. You stop worrying about whether your tone of voice sounds enthusiastic enough.

It makes complete sense that you would want to return to that relief.

It makes sense that you would want to stay in it.

It makes sense that you would want to lock the door and never leave.

Pain as Proof That You Are Still Here

There is something else that happens in the dark. Something harder to say out loud, but important enough to name.

When you have been floating in gray, numb static for a long time, pain itself can start to feel like the only proof that you are still alive.

When everything else feels distant, the ache in your chest is real.

It is something you can feel.

It becomes a strange kind of anchor.

It is not good. It is not healthy. But it is real, and real is something.

Some people find other ways to make that realness sharper. Some people use physical pain to cut through the emotional numbness, to feel something undeniable in a world that has gone completely flat. They use pain to prove they are still here, to force the body to register something, anything, other than the void.

If that is part of your story, I want you to hear this clearly:

This book is not here to shame you.

What you were looking for, proof that you are still here, a way to anchor yourself to reality, is a deeply human need. You were trying to survive the numbness in the only way that made sense at the time.

But this book is also not here to teach you how to hurt yourself.

The dark is already asking too much of you. You deserve help that does not require you to hurt yourself to feel real.

If you are in danger of harming yourself right now, please reach for immediate help. The number 988 will connect you to someone who can sit with you in this moment.

You do not have to carry the numbness alone.

Rest Is Not the Same as Paralysis

The dark offers relief from the performance of life, but we have to be honest about what that relief can become.

The dark is not actually keeping you safe.

It is keeping you still.

There is a profound difference between rest and paralysis.

Rest restores you. Rest is the quiet pause that allows your body and mind to recover enough to meet the next moment.

Paralysis holds you in place while the world moves on without you.

When you first retreat into the dark, it feels like rest. It feels necessary. You are so exhausted by the performance of normalcy that the dark feels like medicine. It feels like finally putting down a weight you have been carrying for miles.

But the longer you stay still, the harder it becomes to imagine moving again.

The heavy blanket stops feeling like a shield and starts feeling like a trap.

The dark may feel like home, but it is not all there is. It is a room you learned to survive in. And the fact that you have learned its rhythms, its numbness, and its strange rules does not mean you were meant to stay there forever.

The Dark Is Not the Whole World

I am not going to ask you to throw off the blanket today.

I am not going to ask you to step out into the bright, loud world and pretend you are ready for it.

You do not have to leave the dark today.

You do not have to leave it this chapter.

But maybe, for now, it is enough to know this:

The dark is not the whole world.

It only feels that way from inside the room.

The familiarity of the dark is a powerful illusion. It convinces you there is nothing else out there, or that whatever is out there is too dangerous to touch. It tells you this room is the only place you will ever belong.

But that is just the dark talking.

It wants to keep you still.

You do not have to fight it today. You do not have to prove it wrong all at once. You only have to acknowledge that the walls of the room are not the edges of the earth.

For Today

You do not have to leave the dark all at once.

It is enough to notice that the dark is not the whole world.

Chapter 3: The Mask You Wear to Survive

You Got Good at Looking Okay

You have gotten very, very good at it.

So good, in fact, that sometimes you even manage to trick yourself for a few minutes.

The smile that arrives just in time, curving your lips before the other person can register the deadness in your eyes. The laugh that sounds genuine enough, pitched at exactly the right volume so no one looks twice. The posture that says, "I am engaged." The nod that says, "I am listening."

You know exactly when to make eye contact and exactly when to look away. You know how to mirror the energy of the room so perfectly that you become almost invisible.

You have built a version of yourself that shows up to work, to family dinners, to social obligations. A version that performs well enough that no one worries too much, and love does not feel quite so risky.

This version of you is highly capable. It remembers birthdays. It asks follow-up questions about other people's lives. It knows how to deflect attention away from its own internal emptiness.

You have been wearing this mask for so long, and adjusting it so constantly, that some days you forget it is there. It has become a second skin, an automatic reflex that slips into place the moment you step out of your front door or answer a phone call.

It is a brilliant piece of engineering, built entirely out of survival instinct.

But living inside that engineering is suffocating.

You are operating a heavy machine from the inside, pulling levers and pushing buttons to make the outside look human, while the real you is trapped in the dark control room, exhausted and unseen.

The machinery is loud.

The control room is very, very quiet.

The Three Words That Hide Everything

It usually starts with three words.

"How are you?" someone asks.

And before your mind can even process the crushing weight in your chest, the exhaustion in your bones, or the fact that it took you an hour just to convince yourself to get out of bed, the mask answers for you.

"I am fine."

Or maybe it is, "Just tired."

Or, "Work has been a lot lately."

These phrases are the currency of the mask. They are socially acceptable, completely unremarkable, and designed to close the conversation before it can begin.

They are the words that keep people walking past you, satisfied that the social contract has been fulfilled.

You say "I am fine" because the alternative requires more than you have.

The alternative might be saying, "I feel like I am drowning in a room full of air."

And then what?

Then you would have to explain. You would have to manage the other person's reaction. You would have to answer follow-up questions. You would have to deal with their sudden shift from casual greeting to deep concern.

That kind of honesty may be important someday.

But today, it may cost more energy than you have available.

So you use the three words that hide everything.

And you keep walking.

Every time you say those words, a tiny, invisible fracture forms between you and the person you are speaking to. You have protected them from the truth, but you have also locked yourself further inside the room. You have successfully avoided a difficult conversation, but you have also reinforced the walls of your own isolation.

That does not mean you did something wrong.

It means you made a survival calculation.

You chose the answer that allowed you to keep moving.

Why the Mask Is Not Dishonesty

People who have never experienced depression often misunderstand the mask.

If they find out how much pain you have been hiding, they might feel betrayed. They might ask, "Why didn't you tell me? Why did you lie? Why did you pretend everything was okay?"

But the mask is not dishonesty.

It is survival.

When you are living with depression, the world does not have a comfortable place for the truth of what you are carrying. People do not know what to do with, "I am not okay, and I do not know how to fix it."

The truth of depression is heavy. It is awkward. It is hard for people to sit with because it does not offer them a simple role.

When you tell the truth, people often panic. They offer solutions you have already tried.

"Have you tried yoga?"

"Have you tried drinking more water?"

"Have you tried just thinking positively?"

They look at you with helpless, frantic worry. And suddenly, you are not just managing your own crushing depression. You are managing their anxiety about your depression.

That is too much weight.

You are already carrying boulders. You cannot carry their worry too.

So you learned, early and well, to give people the version of you they can handle.

The mask protects the people around you from a weight they may not be equipped to carry, and it protects you from the exhausting vulnerability of being truly seen and then deeply misunderstood.

You are not lying to them in some careless or cruel way.

You are triaging your limited energy.

Triage means deciding what has to be handled first when there is not enough strength, time, or capacity to handle everything at once. In this case, you are deciding what truth you can survive sharing today.

Sometimes, "I am fine" is not honesty.

But sometimes, it is protection.

And protection is not the same as deception.

The Cost of Performing Normal

But the mask has a massive, invisible cost.

Every day you wear it, you are spending energy you do not have. The performance of normalcy is exhausting in a way that is almost impossible to explain to someone who has never had to do it.

It is not just the act of smiling.

It is the constant, hyper-vigilant monitoring of your own existence.

You are watching your own face from the inside. You are calibrating your tone so it does not sound too flat. You are making sure you ask follow-up questions so you appear interested. You are calculating exactly how much energy you need to spend to make it through the next hour, the next meeting, the next conversation.

It is a full-time, high-stress job layered directly on top of the already crushing physical and mental weight of depression.

You are running a marathon while pretending you are just taking a casual stroll.

And the hardest part is that no one is clapping for you at the finish line, because no one even knows you are running.

You sit in a meeting at work, nodding along to a presentation, and the amount of concentration it takes just to keep your face arranged in an expression of mild interest is staggering. By the time the meeting is over, you feel like you have been completely drained, but to everyone else, you just look like a person who attended a meeting.

No one sees the effort.

No one sees the calculations.

No one sees how carefully you are holding yourself together.

They only see that you showed up.

And showing up has already cost you almost everything.

When the Mask Comes Off at Home

And then, eventually, you get to go home.

You close the front door.

You lock it.

And the mask drops.

The collapse that follows is not just physical tiredness. It is total depletion. The energy it took to hold the mask up all day has drained whatever small reserves you had left.

You are left aching, hollow, and completely alone with everything you spent the day hiding.

This is the cruel irony of the mask.

It allows you to function in the world, but it leaves you too exhausted to actually live in it. It buys you passage through the day, but the price is your evening, your weekend, your quiet hours, your sense of self.

You spend all your energy pretending to be alive for other people, leaving almost nothing for yourself.

You sit on the couch in the dark, unable to turn on the television, unable to read a book, unable to make a cup of tea. The contrast between the capable, smiling person you were three hours ago and the empty shell you feel like now is terrifying.

You wonder which one is the real you.

And you fear the answer.

The silence of the house is deafening after the loud performance of the day. There is no applause. No witness. No one handing you back the energy you spent.

There is only the quiet.

And the version of you that was waiting underneath the mask.

Being Loved for the Mask

There is something even more painful about the mask, something that cuts much deeper than physical exhaustion.

When people love you, they may be loving the mask.

They love the version of you that shows up, functions, laughs at the jokes, contributes to the project, and seems to be doing fine. They love the low-maintenance, agreeable, performing version of you. They love the person who does not require them to sit in the uncomfortable silence of unresolved pain.

And somewhere in the back of your mind, a quiet and devastating thought takes root:

If they knew the real me, they would not stay.

If they knew the one who cannot get out of bed.

If they knew the one who feels nothing.

If they knew the one who is drowning.

They would leave.

That thought is one of depression's most effective weapons. It feels like the most honest, brutal truth in the world. It convinces you that your true self is unlovable, and that the only way to keep the people you care about is to keep performing.

It tells you that love is conditional on your ability to appear okay.

So you protect the mask even more fiercely.

You maintain it carefully. You make sure no one gets close enough to see the cracks. And in doing so, you become more isolated than ever.

You can be surrounded by a room full of people who care about you and still feel entirely alone, separated from all of them by the very performance you created to keep them close.

This is one of the loneliest parts of depression.

Not being alone.

Being loved, but not feeling known.

You Are Still Behind It

I am not going to tell you to take the mask off today.

I know why you wear it.

I know it keeps you safe.

I know you cannot simply drop it without feeling like the world will crush you.

Taking the mask off requires a level of safety and energy that you may not have right now. It requires a space where the truth will not be met with panic, advice, correction, or demands for immediate improvement.

What I want you to know, for right now, is simply this:

The mask is not who you are.

It is a tool.

It is something you built to survive.

And the fact that you built it, that you had the presence of mind and the sheer endurance to construct something that allowed you to keep functioning in a world that was not built for what you are carrying, says something profound about you.

It says you are resourceful.

It says you are still trying.

It says you are fighting to stay here, even when it takes everything you have.

The mask is not your enemy.

But it is also not your whole story.

Somewhere behind it, underneath the exhaustion and the performance, the real you is still there. Still breathing. Still waiting.

The mask has not erased you.

It has only hidden you for a while.

And that is okay for today.

For Today

The mask is not who you are.

It is just how you survived today.

Chapter 4: When the Light Hurts

The Paradox of the Splinter

There is a strange paradox in depression that is very difficult to explain to someone who has never lived through it.

It is the moment when the dark reality you have been living in is suddenly broken into by something bright.

You might think any intrusion of light into the dark would be a relief. You might think it would feel like rescue. You might assume that when you are drowning in numbness, any spark of genuine emotion would be welcomed like a lifeline thrown into deep water.

But often, it does not feel like rescue at all.

It feels like a splinter.

A splinter is small. Sometimes it is almost invisible. But when it slips under the skin, it demands your attention. It hurts every time you move, every time you brush against it, every time you are reminded that something sharp has lodged itself somewhere tender.

When you are deep in the numbness of depression, a moment of joy, a sudden realization of beauty, or a flash of genuine hope can act exactly like that.

It breaks through the thick, numb barrier you have built to protect yourself. It is a tiny sliver of light, and because it is light, it seems like it should be good. But because it is entering a space that has been dark and numb for so long, it hurts. It disrupts the fragile, flat equilibrium you have managed to create.

It hurts because it is a sharp, sudden reminder of everything you are currently unable to feel for very long. It is a little tease. It shows you a small piece of the world you used to inhabit, but it does not give you the ability to stay there.

You can see it, but you cannot have it.

And that brief glimpse of what you are missing can feel more painful than forgetting what the light looks like altogether.

Witnessing Other People's Joy

This splinter often arrives in the form of other people's joy.

You are walking down the street, feeling the familiar, heavy gravity of the dark, and you see an older couple holding hands, laughing together at some private joke.

Or you are scrolling through your phone and see a video of a clumsy, joyful puppy playing in the grass.

Or you are standing at a family gathering or a child's birthday party, surrounded by bright colors, loud music, and uncontained, chaotic excitement.

For a fraction of a second, the numbness cracks.

You feel a genuine smile start to form.

You feel a brief, startling rush of warmth in your chest.

You remember what it feels like to be part of the world, to be connected to the simple, uncomplicated goodness of a moment.

For a split second, you are back in the land of the living.

And then, almost immediately, the pain hits.

The pain is not because you resent the couple, or the puppy, or the child. You are not angry that they are happy.

The pain comes because that brief flash of warmth highlights the profound coldness of your own internal landscape. It is like turning on a bright, harsh light in a room you have been avoiding for months. Suddenly, you can see all the dust, all the broken furniture, all the vast emptiness the dark had been hiding.

The light illuminates the contrast.

It shows you the distance between the joy happening right in front of you and the vacuum inside your chest. And that distance feels entirely uncrossable.

The joy belongs to them.

The vacuum belongs to you.

And the splinter is the agonizing realization that you do not know how to bridge the gap.

You are watching a language being spoken that you have completely forgotten how to speak.

The Cruelty of the Tease

The splinter of light feels cruel because it feels like a trick.

When you have accepted the dark as your permanent reality, you stop looking for the exit. You settle in. You learn to manage the low expectations. You build a life around the limits of the numbness. You stop hoping for rescue because hoping for rescue takes too much energy.

But when the light breaks in, even for a moment, it forces you to remember what the exit looks like.

It forces you to remember what it feels like to be fully alive.

To have energy.

To feel connection without having to perform your way into it.

And then, just as quickly as it arrived, the light fades.

The joke ends.

The video stops playing.

The party is over.

The heavy blanket of numbness drops back down, often feeling heavier and more suffocating than it did before the light interrupted it. The contrast makes the return to the dark feel like a fresh failure.

This cycle, sudden hope followed by the return of the dark, is exhausting. It is an emotional whiplash that can leave you feeling more depleted than if you had simply stayed numb the entire time.

It is so exhausting that eventually; you may start trying to avoid the light altogether.

You look away from the couple holding hands.

You scroll past the funny videos.

You decline the invitations to the parties.

You protect yourself from anything that might cause that brief, painful crack in the numbness.

You are not avoiding joy because you hate joy.

You are avoiding it because you cannot survive the drop back into the dark.

You are protecting yourself from the splinter. You are choosing the flat, predictable pain of the dark over the sharp, unpredictable pain of hope.

Why You Pull Back from the Light

If you find yourself turning away from the things that used to make you happy, if you find yourself avoiding moments of connection or beauty, I want you to know that this makes sense.

You are not broken because the light hurts.

You are tender where the light is touching.

When something has been injured, even a gentle touch can hurt. A breeze that would normally feel pleasant can sting. Warmth that would normally feel comforting can feel like too much.

Emotional pain can work the same way.

The numbness is not healthy, but it has been doing a job. It has been covering what still feels raw. The light touches that place, and of course you flinch. Of course you pull back. Of course, you protect the part of you that has been exposed too quickly.

So when you pull back from the light, you are not failing.

You are instinctively protecting a very vulnerable part of yourself.

You are managing your pain in the only way that currently makes sense.

You are pulling your hand away from a hot stove, even if the stove is the only source of warmth in the house.

You are doing what humans are wired to do.

You are moving away from the source of the pain.

The Splinter Pause

Later, there is a way to pause with the splinter before it turns into a whole story about your life.

We are not going to practice that yet.

For now, we are only naming the fact that the splinter hurts.

We are not going to force you to hold onto the light today. We are not going to ask you to stare directly into the sun when your eyes have adjusted to the dark. We are not going to hand you a worksheet and tell you to turn that brief moment of joy into a permanent state of mind.

The goal right now is simply to recognize the splinter for what it is.

It is not a punishment.

It is not proof that you are broken.

It is not a trick designed to make you feel worse.

It is a moment of contrast.

When the light breaks in and the pain follows, you do not have to analyze it. You do not have to figure out how to keep the light from fading. You only have to acknowledge that the contrast hurts, and that it makes complete sense that it hurts.

You can say to yourself:

"That was a splinter of light. It hurt because I am in the dark."

And then you can let it be what it is.

You do not have to build a whole narrative around it. You do not have to use it as evidence that you will never be happy again. You do not have to decide that you are fundamentally broken because you could not hold onto a good feeling.

You can let it be a sharp, brief moment.

And then you can go back to resting.

You Do Not Have to Force the Light

The pressure to "be happy" or "look on the bright side" can be enormous.

The world wants you to embrace the light because it makes the world feel more comfortable. People want you to smile because your smile reassures them that their world is safe and functioning properly.

But you do not owe the world your comfort.

You do not owe anyone a performance of joy that you do not feel.

If the light hurts today, you are allowed to close the blinds.

You are allowed to protect your eyes.

You are allowed to say, "Not today."

Healing from depression is not about forcing yourself to stare into the light until you stop wincing. It is about slowly, very slowly, building the internal strength required to tolerate the contrast. It is about eventually reaching a point where the light feels less like a weapon and more like warmth.

But that takes time.

And it takes an immense amount of gentleness with yourself.

For today, if the splinter arrives, just notice it.

Notice that it hurts.

Notice that the hurt is proof that the numbness is not absolute.

The capacity to feel the light, even as pain, means the capacity to feel is still there. You are not broken beyond repair. You are sensitive because something in you is still alive enough to respond.

For Today

You are not broken because the light hurts.

You are allowed to protect your eyes today.

Chapter 5: The Lies That Sound Like You

The Voice in the Room

Depression is not just a physical heaviness.

It is not just the concrete in your veins, the exhaustion in your bones, or the invisible weight pressing you into the bed.

It is also a voice.

And it may be the most convincing, articulate, and devastating voice you will ever hear.

When people talk about the symptoms of depression, they often focus on the physical things: the exhaustion, the changes in appetite, the inability to sleep, the inability to wake up. They talk about the visible markers of the illness, the things that can be measured or observed from the outside.

But the physical symptoms are often only part of what is happening.

There is also the voice.

The voice of depression does not sound like a monster. It does not sound like an external villain trying to trick you. It sounds exactly like you. It uses your vocabulary. It knows your deepest insecurities. It has access to every mistake you have ever made, every time you have ever felt inadequate, every time someone has ever let you down.

Because it sounds like you, and because it has access to your entire history, it does not feel like a symptom of an illness.

It feels like clarity.

It feels like the veil of optimism has finally been lifted, and you are finally seeing the brutal, unvarnished truth about yourself and the world.

When you have a cold, you know the coughing is a symptom. You do not believe that coughing is your true identity. You do not think, "I am cough." You know your body is reacting to something.

But when depression tells you that you are worthless, you may not recognize it as a symptom. You may recognize it as a revelation.

That is part of the cruelty of depression.

It uses your own mind as its primary weapon, turning your intelligence, memory, and sensitivity against you.

It takes the things you are already tender about, your career, your relationships, your body, your past mistakes, your old wounds, and it amplifies them until they are the only things you can see.

It waits for the moments when you are most vulnerable, often late at night or early in the morning, and then it delivers its most devastating arguments.

The Prosecution Rests

Imagine being on trial for a crime you did not commit.

Now imagine that the prosecuting attorney is brilliant.

They have a massive file of evidence against you. They present their case with absolute certainty. They twist every neutral action into a malicious one. They highlight every flaw, every misstep, every time you failed to live up to your own expectations.

Now imagine that you do not have a defense attorney.

And the judge is not neutral.

The judge has already decided you are guilty.

This is what it can feel like to live with the voice of depression. It is a relentless prosecution, and you are too exhausted to mount a defense.

The voice tells you that you are a burden. It tells you that your friends only tolerate you out of pity, and that their unreturned texts are proof that they are finally tired of you. It tells you that your partner would be happier if they were not tethered to your sadness. It tells you that you are fundamentally broken, that you are lazy, that you are selfish, and that the world is moving on without you.

When you hear these things constantly, day after day, in your own voice, you may stop questioning them.

You may start accepting them as facts.

The prosecution rests, and you accept the sentence.

You stop trying to prove your innocence because the sheer volume of evidence the voice presents feels overwhelming. You begin to believe that the dark is exactly what you deserve.

You might even start to agree with the prosecution out loud.

You might apologize constantly for things that are not your fault. You might push people away because you are convinced you are doing them a favor. You might become an active participant in your own trial, helping the prosecution build its case against you.

You stop looking for evidence of your own goodness because the prosecution has convinced you that any goodness is just a temporary illusion.

But remember this:

A courtroom inside depression is not a fair courtroom.

The prosecutor is not honest.

The judge is not neutral.

And the verdict is not the truth.

The Most Dangerous Lie

Of all the lies the voice tells, there is one that needs to be interrupted immediately.

It often comes when the exhaustion is at its absolute peak, when the mask is too heavy to hold up anymore, and when the dark feels like it has swallowed the entire world.

The voice says:

"Everyone would be better off without you."

If that sentence feels true right now, stop here for a moment.

Do not keep reading alone.

Tell someone the lie is talking. Call or text 988 if you might hurt yourself. You do not have to explain your whole life. You only have to let another human being stand between you and the voice for this moment.

That thought is not clarity.

It is not truth.

It is the disease talking through the most exhausted part of you.

It is important to understand how depression constructs this lie, because it does not always present it as self-hatred. Sometimes it presents itself as twisted kindness.

The voice convinces you that your pain is damaging the people you love. It convinces you that your presence is a weight they are forced to carry, a shadow over their lives. It tries to tell you that disappearing would somehow be a gift.

That is how cruel this lie is.

It preys on your love for other people. It uses your empathy as a weapon against you. It takes your desire to protect your loved ones and turns it into a reason to leave them.

If you are hearing this lie right now, I need you to hear me clearly:

It is a lie.

It is not love.

It is not mercy.

It is not a noble conclusion.

It is the ultimate symptom of a nervous system that is completely overwhelmed.

If the voice is telling you that the world would be better without you, please do not listen to it alone. The number 988 is available right now. You do not have to argue with the voice by yourself. Let someone else hold the line for you. Let someone else be the defense attorney for a little while.

You do not have to carry the weight of that lie by yourself.

You only have to let someone else know that the lie is being told.

The Voice Gap

You do not have to argue with the voice today.

You do not have to mount a brilliant defense.

You do not have to prove the prosecution wrong.

Arguing with the voice takes energy, and energy is the one thing you may not have right now. When you try to fight the lies with positive affirmations, the voice may simply present three more pieces of evidence to prove you wrong.

It is a debate you cannot win while you are in the dark.

But if you can notice that it is a voice, that small space matters.

Later, we will call that space the Voice Gap.

The Voice Gap is the tiny, microscopic distance between the thought happening in your head and your belief that the thought is true.

It is the difference between:

“I am a burden.”

and

“I am having the thought that I am a burden.”

That gap may be incredibly small. It might only last for a fraction of a second.

But that gap is the beginning of freedom.

It is the first crack in the absolute certainty of the prosecution. It is the realization that just because the radio is playing in the background does not mean you have to believe the lyrics of the song.

We are not going to practice widening that gap today.

We are not going to ask you to change the station.

For now, it is enough just to notice that the radio is on, and that it is playing a very specific, very cruel song.

You do not have to turn it off.

You just have to recognize that it is a broadcast, not the truth.

Even if the voice is screaming at you, that tiny sliver of awareness, the part of you that realizes the voice is screaming, is proof that the voice is not the entirety of who you are.

The part of you that notices the thought is separate from the thought itself.

That separation is the Voice Gap.

And that gap, no matter how small, is a place where hope can eventually take root.

You Do Not Have to Believe Everything You Think

For today, the only thing you need to do is notice the voice.

When it tells you that you are lazy because you cannot get out of bed, just notice it.

When it tells you that your friends hate you because they have not texted, just notice it.

When it tells you that the dark is the only place you will ever belong, just notice it.

You do not have to fight it.

You only have to remember that a thought is not a fact just because it is in your head.

The voice of depression is a symptom, just like a fever is a symptom of an infection. When you have a high fever, you know your body is under strain. You know your perception may be distorted. Ordinary shadows may look threatening. The room may feel colder or stranger than it really is.

Depression can distort your thoughts in a similar way.

You are allowed to hear the voice without believing it.

You are allowed to let it talk without accepting its conclusions.

You are allowed to let the prosecution present its case while remembering that the trial is not fair.

You are not your thoughts.

You are the person listening to them.

And for today, simply listening without agreeing is enough of a victory.

You do not have to defeat the voice today.

You only have to survive it.

You only have to let it talk without handing over the keys to your reality.

For Today

You do not have to argue with the voice today.

You just have to notice that it is a voice.

Chapter 6: When Help Feels Like Pressure

The Weight of Good Intentions

One of the most isolating parts of depression is not just the darkness itself, but the way other people react to it.

When you are drowning, you might assume a life preserver would be a welcome sight. But when you are in the depths of depression, the life preservers people throw at you often feel like anvils.

The people who love you want to fix you.

It is a natural human instinct. When they see someone they care about in pain, their immediate reaction is to find a solution, offer advice, and pull you out of the hole.

They bring you articles about diet and exercise. They tell you about a new supplement they read about. They suggest you just need to get outside and get some fresh air. They remind you of all the things you have to be grateful for.

Their intentions are good.

They are trying to build a bridge for you to walk across.

But when you are barely surviving, good intentions can feel incredibly heavy. Every suggestion, no matter how gently delivered, can feel like a demand. Every piece of advice can feel like an accusation that you are not trying hard enough. Every reminder of your blessings can feel like a spotlight illuminating your failure to appreciate them.

You are not ungrateful for their love.

You are exhausted by the pressure of their expectations.

You do not have the energy to build the bridge they are describing, let alone walk across it.

This creates a terrible paradox: the very people who are trying to make you feel less alone can end up making you feel more isolated.

You realize they do not understand the nature of the dark you are in. They think you are stuck in a ditch you can climb out of, when in reality, you feel pinned under a collapsed building. They are offering you a ladder when what you really need is an excavation team, or simply someone willing to sit in the rubble with you until the dust settles.

Why "Just Snap Out of It" Hurts So Much

The most painful form of help is the kind that assumes depression is a choice.

It comes in many variations:

"You just need to change your mindset."

"Happiness is a decision."

"You have to force yourself to be positive."

"Other people have it much worse."

These statements hurt because they misunderstand the nature of the illness. They assume you are choosing the dark, that you are actively deciding to stay in bed, that you are simply refusing to look at the bright side.

They imply that your suffering is the result of stubbornness.

If you could just snap out of it, you would have done so a long time ago.

No one chooses to feel like they are made of concrete. No one chooses to lose their connection to the people they love. No one chooses the vacuum in their chest.

The idea that you are doing this to yourself on purpose is deeply insulting to the battle you are fighting every single minute of the day.

When someone tells you to just change your mindset, it can feel like they are telling someone with a broken leg to just walk it off. It invalidates the reality of your pain. It makes you feel invisible, even when they are looking right at you.

And the worst part is, a part of you might start to believe them.

The voice of depression, which we talked about in the last chapter, loves to use these statements as evidence against you.

"See?" the voice says. "Even they think you are just being lazy. Even they know you could fix this if you really wanted to. You are doing this to yourself."

This external invalidation feeds the internal prosecution, making the trial inside your head even harder to survive.

The Exhaustion of Managing Other People's Disappointment

When the help does not work, when the walk outside does not cure you, when the gratitude journal does not lift the fog, when the new supplement changes nothing, you are left with a new burden:

Managing the disappointment of the people who tried to help.

You can see it in their eyes.

You can hear it in their sighs.

They offered you a solution, and you were not fixed by it. Now, on top of the depression, you feel the weight of their frustration. You feel like you are failing them. You feel like a broken project they are tired of trying to repair.

This is why the mask we talked about earlier becomes so necessary.

It is often easier to pretend their help worked, to fake a smile and say you feel a little better, than to deal with the crushing guilt of disappointing them again. You spend your last reserves of energy performing recovery just to give them peace of mind.

This dynamic creates a profound sense of loneliness.

You are surrounded by people who love you, but you cannot let them see the truth because the truth feels too frustrating for them to handle. You become a caretaker for their feelings even when you cannot take care of yourself.

You become responsible for reassuring everyone else that you are trying.

And the energy you desperately need simply to breathe gets siphoned off into making other people feel less helpless.

When the Fixers Become the Problem

Sometimes, the people who love you most become the hardest people to be around.

Not because they are bad people.

Because their need to fix you is louder than their ability to sit with you.

When someone is constantly offering solutions, they may be subtly demanding progress. And when you are in the depths of depression, progress can feel impossible. Survival is the only metric that matters.

But fixers often do not understand survival mode.

They want to see movement. They want to see results. They want proof that their love is helping.

Being around a fixer when you are depressed can feel like being in a room with a ticking clock. You constantly feel like time is running out, like you are taking too long to heal, like their patience is wearing thin.

You start to avoid them, not because you do not love them, but because you cannot afford the energy it takes to be their project.

This avoidance often leads to more misunderstanding.

They may think you are pushing them away because you do not care. But you may be pushing them away because their help feels like a physical weight on your chest, and you are already struggling to breathe.

Their anxiety about your condition becomes another symptom you have to manage.

The Toxicity of "At Least"

Another common form of painful help begins with the words "at least."

"At least you have a good job."

"At least you have a roof over your head."

"At least you are healthy."

These statements are meant to offer perspective. They are meant to remind you that things could be worse.

But when you are depressed, "at least" does not always offer perspective.

It often offers shame.

It tells you that because your external circumstances are fine, your internal agony is unjustified.

Depression does not check your bank account or your relationship status before it moves in. It does not look around your life and decide whether you have enough visible reasons to suffer. It is an internal collapse.

Reminding someone of what they have to be grateful for when they are incapable of feeling gratitude is like reminding someone who is starving that there is food behind a locked glass door.

It only highlights the agony of the disconnect.

You are allowed to be in pain even if your life looks fine on paper.

The darkness does not require a justification.

And you do not owe anyone an apology for suffering when "at least" things are okay.

You Are Allowed to Set Boundaries

You do not have to accept every life preserver thrown at you, especially if it feels like an anvil.

You are allowed to protect your limited energy.

It is okay to tell the people you love that you cannot talk about solutions right now.

It is okay to say:

"I know you want to help, but advice feels like pressure today. I just need you to sit with me. I need you to stop trying to pull me out of the dark and just sit in the dark with me for a minute."

Setting this boundary is incredibly difficult, especially when you are already feeling guilty for being a burden.

But it may be necessary for your survival.

You cannot heal if you are constantly defending yourself against well-meaning demands.

If you cannot say the words out loud, you can show them this chapter. You can let the book do the talking for you. You can let these pages explain that their love is felt, but their solutions are too heavy to carry today.

Surviving Bad Help

When someone offers advice that misses the mark entirely, you do not have to internalize it.

You do not have to let it become another piece of evidence in the trial against you.

You can recognize that their advice may be about their discomfort, not your failure. They may be offering solutions because they cannot tolerate the helplessness of watching you suffer. Their "just snap out of it" may really be a plea:

"Please stop hurting, because I do not know how to fix it, and it scares me."

Understanding this does not make the advice hurt less, but it can change the source of the pain. It moves the failure from your shoulders into the space between you.

You are not failing to be fixed.

They may not understand yet that fixing is not what is required right now.

For today, you do not have to manage their feelings. You do not have to perform recovery. You are allowed to be exactly where you are, even if it makes other people uncomfortable.

You are allowed to let their solutions fall to the floor without picking them up.

You do not have to be easy to help today.

You just have to survive.

For Today

You do not have to manage other people's disappointment today.

You are allowed to let their solutions fall to the floor.

Chapter 7: When Your Body Feels Like a Stranger

The Physical Weight of the Dark

We often talk about depression as a mental illness, a disease of the mind. But anyone who has lived in the dark knows that depression is also a deeply physical experience.

It does not just live in your thoughts.

It lives in your bones, in your muscles, in the way your lungs expand and contract.

When you are depressed, the gravity in the room changes. Everything becomes heavier. The distance from the bed to the bathroom door is no longer ten feet. It is a marathon. The act of lifting a glass of water to your mouth requires a conscious, exhausting calculation of energy.

You are not just tired.

You are physically depleted in a way that can feel cellular.

This is why the advice to "just get some exercise" can feel so absurd. The person saying it may not understand that simply existing in your body right now is already an endurance sport.

You are running a marathon just by keeping your eyes open.

Asking you to go for a run can feel like asking someone who is holding up a collapsing roof to start doing jumping jacks. The sheer physical effort required to maintain your current position is invisible to everyone else.

You might notice that your posture has changed. You might find yourself curling inward, protecting your chest, trying to make yourself as small as possible.

This is not just a metaphor for hiding.

It is a physical reality.

Your body is trying to defend itself against a threat it cannot see, but can still feel in every nerve ending.

The Vacuum in Your Chest

There is a specific physical sensation that often accompanies deep depression.

It is not exactly a pain, though it hurts.

It feels more like a vacuum.

It feels like a literal, physical emptiness in the center of your chest, as if something vital has been scooped out, leaving a hollow space behind.

This vacuum is not passive. It pulls at you. It aches. It feels like the physical form of the numbness we talked about earlier. It is the sensation of feeling nothing so intensely that it becomes painful.

It is an active, demanding void.

People who have never experienced this vacuum may think of emptiness as a metaphor. But you know it can feel tangible. Heavy. Present. Something you carry around with you all day.

You try to breathe around it.

You try to sleep through it.

But it is always there, a constant reminder of the disconnect between you and the world.

Sometimes, the vacuum makes it hard to breathe. You find yourself taking shallow, ragged breaths because a deep breath would require expanding that hollow space, and expanding it hurts. You live on the top layer of your lung capacity, just enough air to survive, but never enough to feel full.

The simple act of breathing becomes work.

The Marionette Feeling

Because your body feels so heavy, and because the vacuum in your chest is so distracting, moving through the world can require a strange kind of distance from yourself.

You stop feeling like you are living in your body.

You start feeling like you are operating it from far away.

You become a marionette, and you are the exhausted puppeteer trying to pull the strings.

You have to consciously tell your arm to reach for the door handle. You have to consciously tell your mouth to form the shape of a smile. You have to consciously command your vocal cords to say, "I am fine."

This mechanical way of moving through the world is incredibly draining.

When every action requires a direct, conscious command, there is no flow. No natural rhythm. No ease. You are constantly micromanaging your own existence just to appear normal to the people around you.

This is why you crash so hard when you finally get back to the safety of your bed.

You drop the strings.

You stop trying to operate the machine.

You let the gravity win for a while.

The relief of no longer having to manually operate your own limbs can be profound. But it can also be frightening, because you wonder if you will ever be able to pick the strings back up again.

The Sensory Distortion

Depression does not just affect your energy.

It can affect your senses.

The world often looks different when you are in the dark. Colors may seem muted, as if someone has turned down the saturation on the screen. Food may lose its taste, becoming only texture, you have to force yourself to swallow.

Sounds can become unbearable.

The hum of the refrigerator. The ticking of a clock. The chatter of people in the next room.

Things that used to be background noise can suddenly feel like physical assaults. Your nervous system is so frayed that ordinary sensory input feels like sandpaper against an open place.

Or the opposite may happen.

You might experience a complete sensory dulling. You might take a shower and barely feel the hot water on your skin. You might wrap yourself in a heavy blanket and still feel exposed to the cold. Your body is present in the room, but your sensory connection to the world feels distant, delayed, or severed.

This distortion makes the physical world feel alien.

You can become a stranger in your own house.

A stranger in your own skin.

You may feel like you cannot trust what you see, hear, or feel, because depression has interfered with the way the world reaches you.

Your Body Is Not Failing You

When your body feels this heavy, when your senses are distorted, when moving feels like operating machinery, it is easy to become angry with yourself.

You look at your hands and wonder why they will not just do the dishes.

You look at your legs and wonder why they will not just walk you out the door.

You feel betrayed by your own physical form.

But your body is not failing you.

Your body is doing what bodies often do under extreme, prolonged stress. It is conserving energy. It is shutting down what it can. It is pulling you toward stillness because the alarm bells in your nervous system have been ringing too loudly for too long.

The exhaustion is not laziness.

The heaviness is not a character flaw.

It is a physical response to an overwhelming internal load. Your body is registering the weight of the dark, and it is trying to keep you alive in the only way it knows how.

If you were carrying a hundred-pound backpack, no one would call you lazy for needing to sit down.

Depression is a hundred-pound backpack that only you can feel.

Your body is responding to the invisible weight it is being forced to carry. It is asking for rest because the load is real, even when no one else can see it.

The Ache of Being Touched

Because your body is in a state of high alert and extreme exhaustion, physical touch can become complicated.

A hug from someone you love, something that might normally feel comforting, can suddenly feel suffocating. The pressure of their arms may feel like an intrusion on your already limited space.

You might flinch when someone touches your shoulder, not because you do not love them, but because your nervous system cannot process the input.

The sensory overload we talked about earlier extends to physical contact.

A gentle touch can feel like a shock.

This creates another layer of guilt. You may want to be comforted, but the physical act of being comforted may feel like too much to bear. You may want the warmth of connection, but your skin feels too raw to accept it.

So you isolate yourself physically, which only deepens the emotional isolation.

It is important to know that this aversion to touch does not make you broken.

A hug can feel like a trap when your nervous system is overwhelmed.

That does not mean you do not love the person offering it.

It means your body is overloaded.

The Ghost of Your Own Energy

Perhaps one of the strangest physical sensations of depression is remembering what it used to feel like to have energy.

You can remember what it felt like to jump out of bed, to run, to dance, to move without calculating the cost. You can remember what it felt like to be spontaneous, to say yes without first checking how much strength was left in your body.

That memory can haunt you.

It is the ghost of your own vitality.

You look at old photographs of yourself and wonder who that person is, because you cannot connect the physical reality of that smiling, active person with the heavy, exhausted body you inhabit now.

Mourning the loss of your own energy is a valid grief.

It is okay to be sad that your body does not feel like yours right now.

It is okay to miss the lightness you used to take for granted.

But remembering that lightness is also proof that the heaviness is not your permanent state. The ghost of your energy is a reminder that the concrete is not your natural form. You may feel trapped in it right now, but you are not made of it.

Honoring the Heaviness

You do not have to fight the gravity today.

You do not have to force the marionette to dance.

You are allowed to acknowledge that your body is carrying an impossible load, and you are allowed to let it rest.

This does not mean you are giving up.

It means you are stopping the war against your own physical reality.

When you stop fighting the heaviness, it does not magically disappear. But it may stop requiring the extra energy it takes to hate yourself for feeling it.

For today, you can notice the vacuum in your chest without trying to fill it. You can notice the concrete in your legs without trying to run. You can allow your body to be exactly as exhausted as it actually is.

You do not have to pretend to be light when today feels made of stone.

Your body has been fighting a silent war for a very long time.

It is allowed to be tired.

You are allowed to be tired.

For Today

You do not have to fight the gravity today.

82

You are allowed to let your body rest.

Chapter 8: One Clean Signal

The Paralysis of the Big Picture

When you are deep in the dark, looking at the "big picture" is not just overwhelming.

It is paralyzing.

If you think about everything it might take to feel normal again, the therapy, the medications, the repairing of relationships, the rebuilding of your career, the re-engaging with life, you may never get out of bed.

The mountain is too high.

And you are too tired to even look at the summit.

This is why most advice fails. It asks you to look at the summit. It asks you to make a five-year plan when you are struggling to survive the next five minutes. It demands a level of cognitive and physical energy that you simply may not possess right now.

To survive this, you have to shrink the timeline.

You have to stop looking at the mountain and start looking at the ground directly in front of your feet. You have to find one tiny, manageable action that does not require hope, does not require a plan, and does not require you to feel better.

You need an action small enough to slip under the radar of your depression.

When your brain tells you that nothing matters, arguing with it is exhausting. The way through is not to argue. The way through is to agree that the big picture is impossible right now, and then do something incredibly small anyway.

You are not trying to change the entire trajectory of your life.

You are only trying to change the physical reality of the next ten minutes.

The Danger of "Just Shower"

If someone tells you to "just take a shower," it can sound incredibly insulting.

To them, a shower is a ten-minute hygiene routine.

To you, a shower is a twenty-step obstacle course.

You have to throw off the blanket. You have to sit up. You have to put your feet on the floor. You have to stand. You have to walk to the bathroom. You have to turn on the water. You have to wait for it to get warm. You have to take off your clothes. You have to step in.

Then you have to wash your hair.

Wash your body.

Turn off the water.

Step out.

Dry off.

Find clean clothes.

Put them on.

When your body feels like concrete, that is not "just a shower."

That is a triathlon.

It requires a sequence of commands from the exhausted puppeteer we talked about earlier. It requires negotiating with gravity at every single step.

So, when we talk about taking a shower here, we are not talking about it the way healthy people talk about it. We are not pretending it is easy. We are acknowledging that it is a monumental effort.

We are asking you to do it anyway, not because it will cure you, but because it serves a very specific purpose.

And we are asking you with full respect for how hard it is.

Interrupting the Static

When you stay in bed for days, your body and your mind can begin to merge into one continuous loop of static.

The sheets smell like your sweat. The room smells like your breath. The air feels heavy. The physical environment becomes an echo chamber for the depression.

You begin to feel indistinguishable from the bed you are lying in.

You need to interrupt that static.

You need to introduce a sensation that is different from the numbness and the ache. You need a shock to the system, but a gentle one. You need to break the continuous loop of sensory deprivation.

This is the purpose of the shower.

The hot water hitting your skin is a physical sensation that depression cannot completely numb. The sound of the water drowning out the silence of the room is an auditory break. The smell of the soap is a sensory input that cuts through the stale air. The act of scrubbing your skin is a physical action that asks the marionette strings to move in a new pattern.

It is not a cure.

It is an interruption.

It is a way of reminding your nervous system that other sensations exist besides the heavy, pulling vacuum in your chest. It proves to your body that it is still capable of feeling something other than pain or numbness.

The Importance of the Soap

It is not enough to just stand under the water.

You have to use soap.

This sounds trivial, but it is actually the most important part of the process.

When you are depressed, you may feel fundamentally unclean. Not just physically, but emotionally and spiritually. You may feel like the darkness has seeped into your pores. You may feel covered in a layer of failure, exhaustion, sweat, and shame.

The physical act of lathering soap and washing it away is a symbolic cleansing. It is a way of physically removing the accumulated sweat and oil of the depression. It is tactile, undeniable proof that your state has changed.

You were unwashed.

Now you are washed.

It is a clear shift in a world that feels entirely gray.

You do not have to feel happy while you do it. You can cry the entire time. You can lean against the tile wall because you are too tired to stand up straight. You can hate every second of it.

The soap does not care about your mood.

It only cares about the friction.

The soap works whether you believe in it or not.

One Clean Signal

This is what we call **One Clean Signal**.

It is the first tool we use when the dark is too thick to navigate.

When your brain is telling you that you are worthless, that you can accomplish nothing, that you are entirely paralyzed, the shower becomes a piece of undeniable, physical evidence to the contrary.

The voice in your head can lie to you about your future, but it cannot lie to you about the fact that you just washed your hair.

The smell of the soap is a fact.

By taking a shower, you are sending one clean signal through the static. You are proving to yourself that you are still capable of action, even if that action is exhausting. You are establishing a tiny place of order in the middle of the chaos.

You are placing one small mark in reality that says:

"I moved."

This is not about building momentum.

It is not about starting your day.

It is simply about proving that the paralysis is not absolute. It is about creating one undeniable fact that depression cannot easily argue with.

When the voice says, "You did nothing today," you can say, "I showered."

It is a small defense.

But it is a real one.

The Permission to Retreat

This is the most crucial part of the One Clean Signal:

Once you are done, you are allowed to go right back to bed.

The shower is not the first step in a productive day.

It is the only step.

If you tell yourself that you have to take a shower and then get dressed and then go to the grocery store and then answer emails, you may never turn on the water. The cognitive load is too high. The mountain becomes visible again, and the paralysis returns.

You must give yourself explicit permission to retreat.

The deal you make with yourself is this:

"I will get up. I will wash my body with soap. I will put on clean clothes. Then I will get back under the covers."

Often, the hardest part of doing anything when you are depressed is the fear of what comes next.

By removing the "next," you make the action possible.

The shower becomes a closed loop. It is an accomplishment that requires no follow-up. You are not starting an engine. You are striking a single match and letting it burn exactly as long as it can.

The Clean Sheets, If You Have Them

If you have a tiny reserve of energy left, and only if you have it, change your sheets before you get back into bed.

Or, better yet, ask someone else to change them while you are in the shower.

If you live with someone, this is a perfect, tangible way for them to help that does not require advice.

Getting a clean body into a clean bed is one of the few physical comforts that can sometimes penetrate the numbness. It creates a physical boundary between the depression of yesterday and the reality of today. It is a way of honoring the effort you just made.

It makes the retreat feel like a choice rather than a defeat.

But if changing the sheets feels like a mountain, leave them.

The clean body is enough.

The One Clean Signal has been sent.

The static has been interrupted.

You have done the hardest thing, and now you are allowed to rest. You are allowed to take the clean signal back into the dark with you.

You Do Not Have to Like It

It is perfectly acceptable to resent the shower.

You do not have to practice gratitude for the hot water. You do not have to pretend it feels like a spa day. You are allowed to be angry that you have to work this hard just to achieve basic hygiene.

The goal is not to change your feelings about the process.

The goal is only to change your physical state.

You can bring all of your anger, all of your exhaustion, and all of your resentment into the bathroom with you.

The water will still run.

The soap will still lather.

This is the beauty of a purely mechanical action. It does not require your emotional cooperation. It only requires your physical presence.

You can be entirely resistant to the idea of getting better, and the soap will still do its job.

For Today

You do not have to build momentum today.

You only have to send one clean signal.

Chapter 9: You Do Not Have to Become the Sun

The Pressure to Heal Overnight

When you finally send that one clean signal, when you finally take that shower or step outside for three minutes, there is often a dangerous expectation that follows.

Both you and the people who love you might secretly hope that this is it. That the fever has broken. That the dark has lifted. That you will now return to your old, radiant self.

This expectation is a trap.

It is the reason so many people give up after taking their first step. When you wake up the next morning and the concrete is still there, it feels like a massive failure.

You think, "I tried, and it did not work. I am still broken."

You have to release yourself from the pressure to heal overnight.

You do not go from living in total darkness to becoming the sun in a single day. You do not even go from total darkness to a well-lit room.

You go from total darkness to a room with a single, flickering candle.

Healing from depression is not a straight line upward. It is not a staircase where every step takes you higher. It is more like walking through a dense forest at night. You might find a clearing where the moonlight shines through, only to step back into the thick trees a few moments later.

The return of the dark does not mean you are failing.

It just means you are still in the forest.

The Flickering Candle

A flickering candle does not illuminate the whole room.

It does not chase away all the shadows.

In fact, it may make the shadows look longer and stranger.

But it is enough light to see your hands. It is enough light to find the door handle. It is enough light to prove that the darkness is not absolute.

This is what recovery can look like in the beginning.

Not a triumphant return to joy.

Not a dramatic transformation.

Not a sudden becoming.

A slow, messy, exhausting accumulation of tiny moments with slightly less pain.

You might have one hour on a Tuesday when the vacuum in your chest feels a little less demanding. You might laugh at a joke on a Thursday and realize, a few seconds later, that it was a genuine laugh. You might take a shower on a Saturday and not feel the immediate need to get back into bed.

These are flickering candles.

They are fragile.

They may go out easily.

You will have days when the dark returns completely and you feel like you have lost all your progress. That is not a failure. That is the nature of the terrain.

The goal is not to keep the candle lit perfectly at all times.

The goal is to remember where the matches are.

The Next Step: Breath and Step Back

As you accumulate these tiny moments, you may eventually need more tools.

The shower is a survival tactic, but it is not a long-term strategy. When you are ready, and only when you are ready, you may need to learn how to sit with the splinter of light without letting it become a whole story about your life.

There is a tool for this.

We call it **Breath and Step Back**.

It is a way of recognizing the light, acknowledging the pain it causes, and then stepping back far enough to observe it without being consumed by it. It is a method for expanding that tiny gap between feeling the pain and becoming the pain.

But we are not going to practice that today.

Today, it is enough just to know the tool exists.

It is enough to know that when you are ready to build the bridge, the blueprints are waiting for you.

For now, you do not have to build the bridge. You do not have to understand the whole design. You do not have to trust your hands to hold the tools yet.

You only have to survive the dark.

The blueprints will still be there when your hands are steady enough to hold them.

The Myth of the "Old You"

One of the heaviest burdens you may be carrying right now is the desire to get back to the "old you."

You remember the person you were before the dark descended. The person who had energy. The person who laughed easily. The person who did not have to calculate the cost of a shower. The person who could say yes without first measuring how much strength was left.

You want that person back.

Of course you do.

But trying to resurrect the old you can become its own kind of despair.

The truth is, you have lived through something profound. The dark changes you. It changes your perspective, your nervous system, and your understanding of pain. It changes what you know about silence, endurance, loneliness, and survival.

You do not have to go backward.

You do not have to un-know what you have learned in the dark.

The goal of recovery is not to erase the experience of depression, as if it never happened. The goal is to integrate it, to carry the truth of what you survived without letting it become the whole definition of who you are.

The person you become on the other side of this may be different from the person you were before.

That does not mean they are ruined.

It means they are real.

Mourning the old you is a necessary part of the process. It is okay to miss the version of yourself who could move through the world with more lightness. It is okay to grieve the ease you used to have.

But do not let the ghost of who you were prevent you from seeing the quiet strength of who you are becoming.

The Courage of Staying

There is a specific kind of courage that rarely gets acknowledged.

It is not the courage of climbing mountains or fighting dragons.

It is the courage of staying present when everything inside you wants to disappear.

When depression is heavy, even staying in the room can feel like a battle. Even breathing can feel like work. Even reading one more page can be an act of endurance.

People who have not lived in the dark may not understand how much courage it takes just to keep going when the air feels like water.

You need to give yourself credit for this courage.

You are not weak for struggling.

You are surviving something most people cannot see.

The fact that you are still here, reading these words, means that some small, stubborn part of you is still resisting the gravity. Honor that part of yourself. It is precious. It may not feel loud. It may not feel inspiring. But it is still here.

When the voice tells you that you are a coward for not being able to face the world, remember the struggle you are carrying internally.

You are not failing because this is hard.

You are enduring something hard.

And the fact that you are still here matters.

The Value of Small Things

As you move forward, you may need to redefine what success looks like.

Success may not look like big achievements right now. It may not look like promotions, grand vacations, perfect relationships, spotless houses, or dramatic reinventions.

Success may look like small things.

Drinking a full glass of water.

Putting on clean socks.

Listening to a song and actually hearing the music.

Letting the sun touch your face for sixty seconds.

These small things are not meaningless just because they are small.

They are the substance of recovery.

They are the moments when life reaches you, even briefly. They are the places where the numbness thins. They are the quiet proof that the dark has not entirely consumed you.

When you learn to value the small things, the pressure of the big picture begins to soften. You stop asking how you will survive the rest of your life, and you focus only on how you will survive the next hour.

That is not a small thing.

That is how people make it through.

The Acceptance of the Gray

Eventually, you may find that the goal is not to eliminate every trace of darkness forever.

The goal may be learning how to live in the gray.

The gray is the space between the blinding light of the sun and the absolute black of the void. It is the place where you can function, connect with others, and find moments of peace, even if the underlying ache is still present.

Living in the gray means learning your own weather.

It means recognizing the early warning signs: the subtle shift in gravity, the faint return of the static, the quiet pull toward isolation. It means learning how to respond before the concrete fully sets.

This acceptance is not defeat.

It is a profound act of self-respect.

It is saying, "I am a person who struggles with this, and I can still be worthy of care. I do not have to be perfect to be worthy of life."

The gray is where the real work of living happens.

It is where you build the bridge.

It is where you learn to carry the weight without letting it define you.

A Quiet Blessing for the Dark

I want to leave you with this:

You are surviving something incredibly difficult.

The fact that you are reading this book, the fact that you are still breathing, the fact that you are still here, is a testament to a quiet, stubborn strength you may not even realize you have.

You are allowed to be tired.

You are allowed to be angry.

You are allowed to be entirely unimpressed with the progress you are making.

You do not owe anyone a performance of recovery.

You do not have to become the sun.

You do not have to radiate joy or positivity or gratitude.

One small candle is enough.

I am sitting here in the dark with you. I know how heavy the blanket is. I know how loud the voice is. I know how far away the rest of the world can feel.

You are not alone in this room.

You are not the only one who has felt this concrete.

You are not broken beyond repair.

You are carrying an impossible weight, and you are doing the best you can.

Just breathe.

Just stay.

Just send one clean signal when you can.

The light will still be there when you are ready for it.

For Today

You do not have to become the sun.

One small candle is enough.

Appendix: When the Dark Is Too Heavy

There will be days when the dark is too heavy to carry alone.

There will be days when the voice is too loud, and the gap between hearing it and believing it disappears completely.

When that happens, you cannot rely on a book.

You need another human being to stand between you and the void.

Please use these resources. You do not have to explain your entire life. You do not have to find perfect words. You only have to let someone help you survive the next ten minutes.

United States

988 Suicide & Crisis Lifeline: Call or text 988. It is free, confidential, and available 24/7.

Crisis Text Line: Text HOME to 741741 to connect with a volunteer Crisis Counselor 24/7.

The Trevor Project, for LGBTQ+ young people: Call 866-488-7386 or text START to 678-678.

Veterans Crisis Line: Dial 988, then press 1, or text 838255.

International

If you are outside the United States, contact your local emergency number or search for crisis services in your country through the International Association for Suicide Prevention, IASP, or another trusted local mental health organization.

Also by Angie G. Ford

The Splinter of Light Series

You have been sitting in the dark, learning the shape of it. But what about the practical tools for building a bridge out?

The Light You Can Reach is the companion guide written for the person who is ready to begin moving toward the light. It introduces the tools named in this book, including The Splinter Pause, The Voice Gap, One Clean Signal, and Breath and Step Back, and shows you how to use them, one small step at a time.

The Light You Can Reach

Practical Tools for Building a Bridge Out of the Dark

Coming soon.

And if someone in your life is trying to support you through depression, they deserve their own guide.

Holding the Light

How to Support Someone with Depression Without Losing Yourself

Coming soon.

The Done List Series

The Done List

Ease Anxiety with Small Daily Wins

The Done List for Loved Ones

How to Support Someone with Anxiety Without Losing Yourself

Fiction

Are You There, God? It's Me, Peggy.

We Were Going to Be Great Mothers

Journals & Trackers

Sweat, Swear, Survive

A Menopause Symptom Tracker for Hot Flashes, Mood Swings, and WTF Moments

All titles available on Amazon.

About the Author

Angie G. Ford writes fiction and nonfiction for women who are living in the middle of things. Her work sits at the intersection of emotional honesty, humor, and the complicated, beautiful lives women actually build.

She is the author of The Done List, The Done List for Loved Ones, We Were Going to Be Great Mothers, Are You There, God? It's Me, Peggy., and Sweat, Swear, Survive. She writes under the Sunflower Phoenix Publishing imprint, a name that carries its own promise: something worth reading can grow from the ground up, and a story told with honesty is always worth telling.

When the Light Hurts is her love letter to anyone who has ever felt like the darkness was permanent, and to the quiet, stubborn strength it takes just to keep breathing.

A Note for Support Groups & Therapy Settings

When the Light Hurts was written to be read alone in the dark, but it was also designed to be discussed in the light.

Healing from depression often requires a community of people who understand the weight of the concrete.

The following questions are designed for therapy groups, support circles, or any gathering of people working together toward understanding and support. The goal is not to fix each other. The goal is to witness each other.

For discussion guides, bulk order inquiries, or support group use, contact Sunflower Phoenix Publishing.

Discussion Questions

1. In Chapter 1, the book distinguishes between sadness as a visitor and depression as the house itself. Does that distinction resonate with your experience? How would you describe the "house" of your depression?

2. The book discusses the strange comfort of the dark, describing it as a place with fewer variables. Have you ever found yourself retreating to the dark because it

felt safer than the unpredictability of the outside world?

3. We talked about the exhaustion of wearing the mask and saying "I am fine" as a way to protect limited energy. What does your mask look like? Who are the people you feel safe taking it off around, if any?

4. The splinter of light is described as painful because it reminds you of what you feel you cannot have. Can you share a time when a moment of hope or joy actually made you feel worse? How do you handle those splinters now?

5. Chapter 5 explores how the voice of depression can sound exactly like your own voice. What are some of the most common lies your voice tells you? How do you practice finding the Voice Gap between hearing the lie and believing it?

6. We discussed why well-meaning advice often feels like an anvil instead of a life preserver. What is the most unhelpful thing someone has said to you? What is the most helpful thing?

7. The concept of One Clean Signal is meant to interrupt the static without requiring a full day of productivity. What is your version of a clean signal?

What small action proves to you that you are still capable of moving?

8. The book ends by giving you permission to not become the sun. What does a flickering candle look like in your life right now? What kind of support helps you protect it without pressure?

NOTES

www.ingramcontent.com/pod-product-compliance
Lightning Source LLC
LaVergne TN
LVHW100329210926
848480LV00003B/1293